Factory Reset

Renewed Thinking That Drives Results

Manny Melendez

FINA PRESS™

Copyright © 2026 Manny Melendez

Published by Fina Press, an imprint of WoW Media Publishing LLC

FINA PRESS™

www.wowmediapublishing.com

Facebook: @wowmediapublishingFB

Instagram: @wowmediapublishinglm

[[CIP DATA HERE]]

ISBN: (Paperback) 978-1-963998-15-3

ISBN: (E-Pub) 978-1-963998-16-0

ISBN: (PDF) 978-1-963998-17-5

Cover design by Lisa McClure of McClure Design

Back cover photo credit: Victor Manuel Melendez

1 2 3 4 5 6 7 8 LSI 33 32 31 30 29 28 27 26

Contents

Chapter 1
The Alignment Multiplier

What's the cost of misalignment in your organization? More than you think. Before strategy, before talent—alignment is the multiplier for every result. Every successful organization runs on a shared objective. Not slogans. Not posters on the wall. Not quarterly hype speeches. A real objective is something people buy into when nobody is watching.

Whether you're leading twelve people in a classroom, twelve hundred on a sales floor, or twelve thousand across global divisions, the principle is the same: If people don't know what they're building **together**, they will default to survival. Survival creates silos. Silos destroy alignment. And once alignment is gone, it doesn't matter how smart your strategy is—execution will fall apart.

FROM SURVIVAL TO OWNERSHIP

Early in my career, I was hired as a telecom trainer. The job came with a warning label: the class had a 50% to 60% failure rate. Not because the company hired the wrong people.

Not because the material was impossible. Most people failed because, under pressure, the test felt bigger than their future. They had information. They had a job. But they didn't have a vision that connected this class to their life in a meaningful way.

On my very first day standing in front of those twelve students, I was nervous. I won't sugarcoat it. I'm from Jersey—we speak fast, think fast, and get right to the point—but that day I felt the weight of responsibility. I wasn't just teaching systems. I was stepping into a room filled with people carrying fear, doubt, pressure, bills, families, and expectations.

So instead of starting with policy manuals and technical slides, I did something different. I reset the room. I asked questions. Not corporate questions—human ones. Why are you here? What are you trying to change in your life? What's the real reason you took this job?

As the icebreakers unfolded and the stories surfaced, a pattern hit me like a brick wall. Not one person in that room owned a home. Not a single one. And right there—standing in front of a group with talent, drive, and pressure stacked against them—I realized something: They didn't need more pressure. They needed a bigger vision.

So, I threw the script out. I said, "What if passing this class isn't the real goal?" Heads lifted. "What if the goal is home ownership?" Silence. Not cars. Not watches. Not lifestyle flexing. Homes. Stability. Legacy.

That day, we made a pact. We would study together. Struggle together. Compete together. Win together. And I made them a deal. Every week during lunch, I would bring in someone from outside the company: a realtor one week, a mortgage broker the next, a credit repair specialist after that. No hype. Just knowledge.

The class objective officially stayed the same—deliver quality service to customers—but now there was a deeper meaning attached to every call they took. Serve correctly. Earn honestly. Build ownership. Suddenly, this wasn't about passing a test to keep a job; this was about rewriting a future. They weren't just trainees anymore. They were future homeowners in training.

FROM CLASSROOM TO BOARDROOM

What happened next wasn't magic—it was alignment. Performance changed. Energy changed. Standards changed. They stopped seeing callers as interruptions—and started seeing them as the source of transformation. Every properly handled call meant compensation. Every check meant progress. Every month meant momentum toward ownership. They reset the way they thought. They rebuilt how they worked. They revealed what discipline produces when it's connected to vision.

When the class ended, I walked them onto the production floor. They didn't just survive—they thrived. A few months later, I got a job offer miles away, and I took it. Life moved on. I assumed that season had closed. Until one year later, my phone rang. "Manny—it's Maria." Maria was one of my students. She said, "I just bought my house." I smiled and congratulated her. Then she said something I will never forget: "You're on speakerphone... I was the last one." And then I heard it. Twelve voices. Cheering. Laughing. Crying. Every single one of them had become homeowners.

In that moment, standing alone in my office in South Florida, I realized something that would shape the rest of my leadership philosophy: People don't fail because they can't learn. They fail when no one has connected their effort to a future that feels worth uniting for. That class didn't pass because the curriculum changed. They passed because their identity changed. Their objective changed. Their sense of who they were building for changed.

LEADERSHIP THAT UNITES

And here's where leadership enters the room. A boss makes sure you do your function. A leader gives you a reason so strong that you *want* to do what they need you to do. A boss says, "Hit your numbers." A leader says, "Here's what we're building—and here's where you fit in." A boss manages tasks. A leader stewards vision.

In that classroom, I wasn't their boss. I didn't control their paychecks or their promotions. But the moment we attached their daily grind to home ownership; I stepped into leadership. I helped them see that this class wasn't separate from their life— it was the bridge to the life they wanted.

SCALING ALIGNMENT: FROM TEAMS TO ENTERPRISES

Now scale that out. If vision can unite twelve people in a training room, what can it do inside a global organization? What happens when: Operations understands how their precision protects the customer promise created by sales? Finance sees themselves as fuel for innovation, not just gatekeepers of cost? Product, marketing, and service all see every launch as one coordinated move, not three separate projects?

Most large organizations don't suffer from a shortage of leadership titles. They suffer from a shortage of shared vision. Departments without a common objective become kingdoms.

Kingdoms without alignment become competition. And internal competition eventually beats the organization before the market ever does.

The real work of leadership in a large organization is not adding more goals. It's clarifying the one objective that makes every team's work matter.

THE BLUEPRINT: CRAFTING YOUR COMMON OBJECTIVE

In that telecom class, the shared objective was simple but powerful: Homeownership. In your organization, the shared objective might sound like:

- "Become the most trusted partner in our industry."
- "Simplify life for our customers in ways no one else will."
- "Turn every customer interaction into a moment of loyalty."

The words are yours to define. But the structure is universal:

- Big enough to unite divisions
- Clear enough to guide decisions
- Personal enough that people can see themselves inside it

This is what *Factory Reset* really means at scale: Not wiping skills. Not deleting experience. Not abandoning structure. It means renewing the operating system of the mind—first at the individual level, then at the team level, and ultimately at the organizational level. A reset doesn't destroy the machine. It prepares it for greater output.

KEY TAKEAWAYS

- **Alignment is the multiplier for every result:** True organizational success starts with everyone sharing a real objective, not just slogans or hype.

- **Survival mode creates silos:** When people don't know what they're building together, they default to survival, which leads to silos and destroys alignment.

- **Vision connects effort to a meaningful future:** People perform better when their daily work is linked to a bigger vision that matters to them personally.

- **Leadership is about uniting people around purpose:** Leaders inspire by connecting tasks to a larger vision, not just by managing functions or numbers.

- **Shared vision breaks down silos and internal competition:** Departments aligned to a common objective work together, strengthening the organization against external challenges.

- **Craft a common objective that is:**
  - Big enough to unite divisions

- Clear enough to guide decisions

- Personal enough for people to see themselves in it.

- **A "Factory Reset" means renewing mindsets:** It's about updating the operating system of the organization—starting with individuals, then teams, and finally the whole enterprise.

Next, we'll explore the "Operating System of Leadership," which will reveal how leaders can update the underlying mindsets, habits, and systems that shape every decision and interaction. You'll discover practical strategies for building a leadership culture that continually resets, adapts, and aligns—preparing your organization for greater output and resilience in a rapidly changing world.

Are you ready to upgrade your leadership operating system? Let's turn the page and begin.

Chapter 2
The Operating System of Leadership

Let's be clear from the start: I'm not writing this as someone who's "figured it all out." I'm a leader in my fifties who has broken things, rebuilt things, and finally started paying attention to the patterns beneath it all. I'm from New Jersey. I'm Puerto Rican. I talk fast, feel deep, and I've lived long enough to know this: Wanting change and thinking differently are not the same thing.

In business, as in life, there are seasons when you know you need a new direction. You feel it in your chest. You realize, "I can't keep doing it like this." But if you're still using the same thinking that built the situation you're trying to escape, you'll stay stuck—not for lack of effort, but because of mindset.

THE LEADERSHIP PIVOT: YOU NEED NEW INPUT

When you genuinely want to pivot—to lead differently, live differently, show up differently—you can't do it alone in your head. You need new input:

- A leader whose vision stretches you

- People who already operate at the level you aspire to
- Environments that challenge your status quo

Real change needs friction. You have to collide with a different way of thinking.

For me, one collision was a program in California called Warrior Week—a no-nonsense, high-integrity, leadership pressure-cooker. They weren't selling hype. They demanded ownership.

THE FACTORY RESET MOMENT

For a long time, Warrior Week was something I circled around. I heard the stories. I saw people come back sharper, clearer, more intentional. But I didn't need another inspirational quote or another "one day I'm gonna…" speech. I needed to be in a room that would call out the gap between who I said I was and how I showed up.

One day, I stopped circling. No big announcement. No dramatic post. I picked up the phone, called, and set up the interview. Simple. Quiet. But that call was a factory reset moment. The second I committed to resetting my mind, my old way of thinking lost its hiding place.

WHEN YOUR INTERNAL STORY GETS TESTED

Warrior Week was one of the toughest things I've done—physically, mentally, emotionally. Not Instagram-tough. Long days. Short sleep. No room for excuses. Everything was designed to test more than your body. They were testing your patterns:

- How you respond under pressure
- How fast you quit
- How honest you are with yourself when nobody's watching

At one point, deep into a drill, my mind started negotiating: "You've done enough." "Slow down, nobody will notice." "You're not built for this anyway." That inner lawyer showed up with a briefcase. Then a coach walked over—calm, locked in—and dropped a line that sliced through my story: "Stop narrating. Finish what you started. The people who depend on you need that version of you."

That hit harder than the drill. It wasn't about the exercise anymore. It was about my operating system—the story running in the background versus the standard I claimed to live by.

NEVER CONFUSE ACTIVITY WITH PRODUCTIVITY

Another line from Warrior Week branded itself on my mind: "Never confuse activity with productivity."

You can run in circles all day and still get nowhere. You can burn energy and make zero progress. You can look committed and still be hiding from the real work. That's not just about drills. That's about business.

Walk into almost any organization and you'll find:

- Calendars packed
- Slack buzzing
- Emails flying
- Everyone "busy"

But busy and effective are not the same. Activity is motion. Productivity is movement that matters.

Warrior Week forced me to see how often I equated "I'm tired" with "I must be productive." That's not just a schedule problem. That's an operating system problem.

THE OPERATING SYSTEM OF LEADERSHIP

Every phone, every laptop, every complex machine runs on an operating system. You don't see it, but it runs everything you do see. Your mind has one, too. It's shaped by:

- Where you grew up
- What you saw in your family
- The leaders you followed

- The environments you've worked in
- The stories you repeat about who you are and what's possible for you

Most people never question that system. They just add new "apps"—new tools, new strategies, new platforms, new initiatives. But the same old operating system is still running underneath—with the same fears, same defaults, same excuses.

At Warrior Week, my mind was exposed. I genuinely valued growth. I wanted to be a better leader. But under pressure, my default was to negotiate with discomfort. In daily life, I wore busyness like a badge and called it progress. I wasn't lazy. I wasn't faking. I was just running an outdated operating system that said: "Good intentions + a full schedule = enough."

But good intentions don't change outcomes. And a packed day doesn't guarantee progress. It just makes you feel justified staying exactly where you are.

THE ILLUSION OF PROGRESS

Sometimes your mind protects you from the truth by creating an illusion of it. One way that the mind does that is by keeping you busy, so you don't have to be honest with yourself.

For individuals, that looks like:

- Researching instead of starting
- Talking about what you're going to do instead of doing it
- Filling your day with low-risk tasks that feel important but don't move the big rocks

For organizations, it looks like:

- Meetings that review the same data week after week
- Strategy decks that never make it to implementation
- "Transformation initiatives" that change logos, not behavior

Everyone's moving. Nobody's advancing. Talking about change—and staying nonstop busy around it—creates a fake sense of momentum. If the thinking underneath doesn't shift, the operating system stays the same. So do the results.

"Never confuse activity with productivity" isn't just a great quote. It's a leadership filter. Ask yourself:

- Does this meeting lead to a real decision?
- Does this project push us closer to our common objective?
- Does this report change what we do on Monday—or just describe what we already know?

If the answer is no, it's noise and activity dressed up like progress.

RESET AT THE INDIVIDUAL LEVEL

Warrior Week didn't turn me into a flawless superhero. That's not how life works. What it did was take away my ability to lie to myself about cetain things. It forced a reset—not in my personality, but in my alignment.

The questions in my head started to change:

- From: "Do I mean well?" "Am I busy?"
- To: "Does my calendar match what I say I value?" "When it gets uncomfortable, do I finish—or do I narrate?" "If I say people depend on me, can they actually depend on my follow-through?" "Am I productive—or just active?"

There's a quiet power that comes when you decide: "From now on, my actions and my words are going to match—and the work I do is going to matter." No press release. No big speech. Just a personal operating standard. That's a factory reset at the individual level: You move from "I'm the kind of person who talks about change," to "I'm the kind of person who follows through."

RESET AT THE ORGANIZATIONAL LEVEL

Now, zoom out. Everything I just said about a person applies to a company. Every organization has an operating system too—not in IT, but in the culture.

It shows up in the sentences people say when the executives aren't in the room:

- "That's just how we do it here."
- "Don't rock the boat."
- "We say we're innovative, but we don't take real risks."
- "We talk collaboration, but every department protects its own scoreboard."

You can change the org chart, roll out a new tech stack, rebrand the website—and still have the same operating system underneath. Same fears. Same silos. Same invisible rules.

A real factory reset in a company starts when leaders are willing to ask uncomfortable questions:

- What do we reward here—talk or execution?
- Where are we confusing activity (being busy) with productivity (creating value)?
- Where do we say, "people first" but behave "politics first"?
- Where are we demanding transformation from teams without modeling it at the top?

Leaders who get this don't just send out new priorities via email. They live a different operating system in front of everybody. They:

- Commit before they communicate
- Own their part before they inspect someone else's
- Show discipline before they demand it
- Measure productivity, not just motion

People watch more than they listen. And they'll end up running on your OS, whether you like it or not.

FROM NOISE TO INTEGRITY

The hardest part of Warrior Week wasn't the physical grind. It was the mirror. It showed me the gap between the version of myself I liked to believe in… and the version that showed up under pressure. Out of that, integrity took on a deeper meaning for me. Not just: "I tell the truth." But: "I live in alignment."

Alignment between:

- What I say and what I do
- What I expect and what I model
- The story I tell about my leadership and the way people experience me

In a corporate setting, that kind of integrity is contagious. If your team sees you start big initiatives and let them quietly die, change priorities every quarter with no explanation, or reward people who look busy over people who get results—they'll copy that OS.

If they see you commit quietly, do hard work without needing applause, finish what you start, call out useless activity and champion real productivity—they will move differently. That's how a reset spreads—from one leader to one team, to an entire culture.

QUESTIONS FOR LEADERS AND TEAMS

You don't need Warrior Week to start this. You just need honesty and a willingness to step into new conversations and new rooms. Here are a few questions to sit with—personally and as a team:

- Where have you been talking about change more than living it?
- Where are you confusing activity with productivity—in your own life and in your organization?
- Who do you need to get around—mentors, leaders, teams— that already operate at the level you say you're aiming for?
- What one specific action can you take this week that sends a clear signal: "We don't just move. We move with purpose."

Factory Reset doesn't start with a campaign or a tagline. It starts the moment you say: "We will not be defined by what we say we want, or how busy we look. We will be defined by what we consistently build."

In the next chapter, we'll talk about guarding vision—how to protect the reset from noise, timing mistakes, and overexposure, so what you're building has a chance to grow roots before it goes public.

KEY TAKEAWAYS

1. Mindset Drives Results

- Change begins with a shift in thinking, not just effort. Leaders must recognize when their current mindset is keeping them stuck and actively seek new perspectives and input.

2. Surround Yourself with Growth

- Progress requires friction—leaders should intentionally place themselves in environments and among people who challenge their assumptions and push them to higher standards.

3. Commitment Triggers Transformation

- Real transformation starts with a quiet, personal commitment—not public declarations. Once you commit, old patterns lose their grip.

4. Test Your Operating System

- Leadership is tested under pressure. Pay attention to your
  default responses and internal narratives—these reveal the
  "operating system" that drives your decisions and behaviors.

5. Activity ≠ Productivity

- Don't mistake busyness for effectiveness. Leaders must dis-
  tinguish between motion and meaningful progress, both personally and organizationally. Ask: Are our actions moving us
  forward, or just keeping us busy?

6. Question Your Defaults

- Most people and organizations run on unexamined habits and stories. Leaders should regularly audit their own and
  their company's "operating system" to ensure it aligns with
  desired outcomes.

7. Beware the Illusion of Progress

- Filling calendars and launching initiatives doesn't guarantee
  advancement. Leaders must challenge activities that create
  a false sense of momentum and focus on what truly drives
  results.

8. Reset Means Alignment

- A true reset is about aligning actions with values and words. Leaders should move from talking about change to consistently following through.

9. Culture Is the Company's OS

- Organizational culture is the invisible operating system. Changing structures or tools won't matter unless leaders begin to model new behaviors and reward execution over talk.

10. Integrity Is Contagious

- Teams emulate what leaders do, not just what they say. Living in alignment—matching expectations with actions—creates a ripple effect throughout the organization.

11. Ask Hard Questions

- Leaders should regularly reflect and challenge themselves and their teams:

  - Are we living change, or just talking about it?

  - Are we confusing activity with productivity?

  - Who can we learn from to reach the next level?

  - What action signals purposeful movement this week?

FINAL THOUGHT

A factory reset for leaders and organizations doesn't start with a campaign or a tagline—it starts with a decision to be defined by what you consistently build, not just what you say or how busy you look.

Chapter 3
Quiet Work, Loud Results

L et's imagine a candid conversation at a kitchen table late at night, where the beer grows warm as the discussion deepens. In today's environment, recognition is often sought before meaningful work is accomplished. New ideas are announced, bold initiatives are introduced, and leadership frequently alludes to grand visions that may never materialize. Applause is given for beginnings, not for completions.

True transformation does not begin with fanfare. It starts with individual, disciplined action—quietly, away from the spotlight. Character is forged in these silent moments, and it is character that sustains progress under pressure.

THE NOISE TRAP

Previous chapters addressed the importance of a shared objective and the mental operating system. Now, we examine the impact of excessive communication. Even with the right goals and mindset, progress can be undermined by speaking more than acting. This challenge is particularly acute for leaders, who are expected to provide constant commentary.

Leaders may fall into the habit of publicly discussing unrefined ideas, sharing concepts before they are tested, and promoting future plans rather than honoring completed work This behavior can create the illusion of leadership and momentum, but risks shifting focus from building reality to managing perception.

The more we speak about unaccomplished tasks, the more personal credibility erodes. Confidence diminishes not because of external criticism, but due to internal recognition of unfulfilled promises.

QUIET DOESN'T MEAN PASSIVE

For years, I kept saying I'd go to Warrior Week. I even wore the t-shirt—but talking about it was a way to feel like I was taking action without ever really stepping up. The truth is, no amount of talk adds up to change. Real progress only started when I stopped performing for others and made the actual commitment. There's a world of difference between talking about what you'll do and just doing it.

Quiet work doesn't mean you're sitting back, letting life happen. It's about being intentional—building before announcing, asking for input from the people who really matter, and caring more about results than appearances. Fear will try to keep you in the shadows or push you to talk just to prove you're in the game. But focus pulls you back to what counts: knowing when to show up and when to just get to work.

There's a kind of freedom that comes with quiet work. It's accountability, not for show, but because you know that when you speak, you've got something to show for it. The basics never change: you get out what you put in, and excuses never move the needle. Quiet work is a lot like planting seeds—at first, there's nothing to see or celebrate. But show up, keep at it, and before long, the results are there for everyone.

In any team or company, quiet work is fixing what others ignore, preparing people for what's next, and keeping systems humming so problems don't pop up later. These behind-the-scenes efforts build trust, create new chances, and widen your influence—not with big gestures, but through steady, consistent action.

So as we move into the next section, I want to look at how all these unseen efforts lay the foundation for real results. In a world that's always talking, it's the quiet work that sets us up for wins that last.

QUIET WORK IN A CORPORATE WORLD

There are periods when talk outweighs action, resulting in stagnation. The most respected seasons are those marked by restraint, self-validation, and living the principles before publicizing them. These foundational efforts, though often unnoticed, underpin future success.

Organizations typically feature two archetypes: the Broadcaster, who excels at communication but may lack substantive impact, and the Builder, whose quiet contributions are integral to operational success. While communication and alignment are vital, cultures that reward broadcasters over builder's risk prioritizing appearance over effectiveness.

Leadership must shift recognition from those who sound like leaders to those who consistently deliver results.

QUIET WORK ≠ LONE WOLF

Premature declarations provide a fleeting sense of accomplishment, but do not equate to genuine progress. Quiet work rejects this early validation, focusing instead on consistent effort and delayed recognition. This discipline shapes not only performance but also character.

Quiet work should not be confused with secrecy or isolation. Strategic communication with relevant stakeholders is essential to prevent misalignment and duplication of effort. The goal is intentional visibility, ensuring the right people are informed at the appropriate time.

LOUD RESULTS

Choosing quiet work does not mean settling for modest outcomes. Instead, it produces results that speak volumes— improved retention, streamlined processes, and cohesive teams. These achievements warrant recognition and serve as evidence of effective leadership.

LEADER CHECK: PREVIEW OR PRODUCE?

Leaders must reflect on whether they invest more energy in discussing culture than modeling it, issuing slogans rather than removing obstacles, and making promises rather than delivering results. Honest self-assessment signals the need for a reset.

SHIFTING FROM BROADCAST TO BUILD

Transformation does not require grand gestures. It begins with clear decisions and disciplined routines. The recommended approach includes:

1. **Define before declaring:** Clarify objectives, relevance, and success metrics.
2. **Make a quiet contract:** Document commitments, timelines, and responsibilities.
3. **Protect a build window:** Dedicate time for design, testing, and early wins.
4. **Communicate proof, not just plans:** Share tangible progress and ongoing challenges.
5. **Let consistency speak:** Build a reputation for reliable execution.

After years of watching teams get caught in the noise—announcing plans, chasing recognition, and mistaking motion for progress—I realized that the real work happens in the quiet. But recognizing where you're broadcasting more than building isn't always obvious in the moment.

That's why I created the Quiet Work Inventory. Use this tools to step back, take stock, and identify the places where disciplined execution will make the loudest impact.

QUIET WORK INVENTORY

Conclude with introspection: Where are you broadcasting more than building? What requires a season of disciplined execution? Who are the quiet builders on your team, and how can you support them? What would change if completed work became the loudest presence in your culture?

Ultimately, loud plans may impress momentarily, but quiet work creates enduring impact.

In the next chapter, we'll talk about Guarding the Vision—how to protect what you're building from wrong voices, bad timing, and premature exposure, so the thing you're working on in the quiet has a real chance to grow strong before it goes public.

KEY TAKEAWAYS

- Recognition follows results, not intentions.
- Quiet, disciplined work builds trust and credibility.
- Announcing plans isn't progress—delivery is.
- Leadership is measured by consistent execution.
- Strategic communication keeps teams aligned.
- Results are the true measure of effectiveness.
- Change starts with clear decisions and routines.
- Support and recognize quiet builders.
- Lasting impact comes from disciplined, quiet work.

Chapter 4
Guarding the Vision

L et's stay at that kitchen table for a minute. Late night. The house is quiet. The beer's getting warm. Because this chapter is about the stuff you don't post—the part of the Factory Reset that happens in your chest before it ever hits your calendar, your strategy deck, or your quarterly goals. We're talking about vision—the kind that moves organizations, not just individuals.

VISION: THE REAL ENGINE OF CHANGE

Vision isn't a bullet point on a slide or a slogan on a wall. It's that picture of "what could be" that grabs you when you're alone, and it's the spark that can ignite a team, a division, or a whole company.

Most real vision doesn't arrive with fireworks. It shows up small—maybe while you're driving, or stirring a pot of rice, or sitting in a meeting where the same problems keep resurfacing. Suddenly, you see a version of your organization that's sharper, more aligned, more impactful. That's vision. Not just goals. Not just "we should do better." Vision is the pull toward something better, something higher, something more honest—for you and for your business.

THE LEADERSHIP TRAP: TALKING VS. BUILDING

Here's where leaders get tripped up. Talking about vision feels good. Say it out loud— "This year, I'm going to lead differently." "We're going to flip this division." "I'm building something new with my team."

You get a rush. Your brain rewards you for saying it. But here's the problem: your brain doesn't always know the difference between *talking about* a thing and *moving toward* a thing. You can stand in a room, announce your new path, and get the nods, the "That's powerful," the "We're with you."

But nothing has changed in your systems, your schedule, your habits, your leadership. It's like eating dessert before you cook the meal. Feels good in the moment. Leaves you with nothing real on the table. If you're not careful, you'll talk your vision to death before it ever has a chance to live.

WORDS ARE THE STEERING WHEEL, NOT THE ENGINE

Words matter. They set direction, align minds, and signal intent. But words are the *steering wheel*, not the engine. The engine is discipline, structure, sacrifice, repetition, and decisions that cost you something. So yes—speak it. Call it out. Point the wheel. But if you never start the engine, you're just sitting in a parked car talking about the highway. Some leaders don't need more declarations. They need some receipts.

THREE CIRCLES OF VISION: A FRAMEWORK FOR LEADERS

Every vision has vulnerable points where it can quietly leak away if you're not intentional. Vision leaks when you share it with people who only know how to criticize, not contribute; when you announce it in big rooms before you've lived it out in small ones; or when you share details just to sound profound, rather than actually build something real. Each time you let vision seep out in the wrong setting, you lose a little of its internal power. Vision rarely dies with a single dramatic failure—it fades with a hundred small leaks.

Guarding your vision doesn't mean you never talk about it—it means you know who to talk to and when. Picture your vision in three circles:

- Circle One – Just You: This is where the vision is born. Sit with it first—don't rush to sell it.
- Circle Two – Your Inner Group: A handful of trusted advisors who will speak truth, want your best, and know your world enough to pressure-test your idea.
- Circle Three – Everyone Else: The wider organization, the market, the crowd. Too many leaders sabotage their own vision by leaping from Circle One straight to Circle Three, skipping the difficult work of testing, refining, and ensuring the vision aligns with who they are and what their company can shoulder.

Honor these circles. Write the vision, wrestle with it, test it, then share it only when it's strong enough to survive opinions, fear, and misunderstanding.

Let your words guide, but let your actions prove your commitment. Some leaders don't even have to announce their vision—the people paying attention can sense it in the way they've changed: how they interact, what they tolerate, how they respond to pressure. You don't have to label it; the ones who "get it" will notice. Everyone else will simply recognize that there's something different about the way you lead.

This systematic approach is crucial, because the true test comes not in the rollout, but in the rhythm of how vision is guarded and lived daily.

ORGANIZATIONAL ALIGNMENT: AVOID OVER-EXPOSING VISION

Organizations often fall into the same trap. They roll out big slogans, host town halls, launch new posters, and unveil glossy presentation decks. Yet beneath all the fanfare, the real drivers—incentives and systems—don't budge. Employees notice the disconnect between what's promised and what's practiced, quietly filing it away: "Nice story. We've seen this before."
So, if you truly want to guard your company's vision, it means more than just words—it calls for real action:

- Don't put words on the wall you're not willing to fight for in real life.
- Don't ask people to clap for a future you aren't constructing.
- Don't force employees to pretend they believe what your systems prove you don't. If you're going to say it, be ready to pay for it—in time, resources, and hard decisions.

Every serious vision deserves a private fight before it ever gets a public stage. Before you put it on slides, put it in a small room with people who don't scare easy. Ask:

- "If we really lived this, what would it cost?"
- "Who in leadership would have to change first?"
- "What current habits, meetings, or metrics would this vision expose?" If the answer is "nothing," it's not vision. It's marketing. Invite challenge in the right place, at the right time, so the vision grows up before you send it out.

THE RHYTHM OF A GUARDED VISION

A guarded vision has a different rhythm than hype. Hype goes: See it. Say it big. Crash later. Guarded vision goes:

- **See it.** Notice what needs to change.
- **Sit with it.** Let it marinate.
- **Share it small.** Bring it to two or three people who will tell you the truth.
- **Start building.** Quietly adjust your own habits, your calendar, one process, one pilot project.
- **Then speak—backed by evidence.** When you bring it to the bigger room, show what's already started, what it's cost, and what you're inviting others into. That's a whole different kind of authority.

If you're leading—at home, at work, in a room, on a call— sit with this:

- Do I share vision to align people or to feel powerful?
- Have I become addicted to the emotional high of talking about change?
- Where have I leaked vision into rooms that weren't ready for it—or that I wasn't ready to back up?
- Have I announced things that my character, habits, or systems weren't ready to sustain?
- Is there a vision I need to stop performing and start protecting and building? That sting you might feel? That's not judgment. That's your integrity waking up.

HOW TO GUARD THE VISION WITHOUT GOING SILENT

Here's how to start guarding vision in a healthy way:

1. Write it for you first. Don't start with a slide deck. Start with a rough, honest version—just for you.
2. Choose your inner circle on purpose. Not just your friends. Not just people who need you to stay the same. Pick those who will challenge and ground you.
3. Build one small piece quietly. Don't wait for the full roll-out. Ask: "What is one behavior, one system, or one project that would make this vision real in a small way?" Do that.
4. Share with receipts. When you talk to the larger group, show what already changed, what you learned, and what's next.
5. Keep a part of it between you and the vision. Not everything needs explaining. Some things are meant to be walked out quietly. The people who are supposed to see it will.

See the tool labeled, "Guarding the Vision: Leadership Checklist" at the end of the chapter to help you apply the concepts.

REFLECTION: TURNING DOWN THE VOLUME, TURNING UP THE WEIGHT

Take a moment. Forget the crowd. Back to the kitchen table. Ask yourself:

- What vision have I been talking about more than building?
- Where am I chasing the feeling of change instead of doing the work of change?
- Who are the two or three people I can trust to help pressure-test what I see?
- What's one vision I need to pull back from the public and quietly start constructing in private? A guarded vision is not a weak vision. It's a protected one. And protected visions—the ones you honor, sit with, refine, and quietly build around—are the ones that survive, serve people, and outlast your job title.

KEY TAKEAWAYS

- **Vision is the catalyst for meaningful change**—but it must be protected, refined, and backed by disciplined execution to drive organizational results.
- **Talking about vision feels rewarding, but action is what delivers impact.** Avoid the trap of over-communicating intent without operational follow-through.
- **Guard your vision by sharing it intentionally:** Start with self-reflection, then test with trusted advisors, and only then communicate broadly.
- **Model the change you want to see.** Leadership credibility is built through consistent behaviors, not just words.
- **Align systems and incentives with vision.** Ensure that organizational structures support the vision, or risk eroding trust and engagement.

- **Pressure-test vision before public rollout.** Use pilot projects and confidential feedback to strengthen ideas and anticipate challenges.
- **Adopt a rhythm of guarded vision:** See it, sit with it, share it small, build quietly, and then communicate with evidence.
- **Reflect regularly:** Use the provided questions to assess whether you're protecting or performing your vision, and adjust your approach accordingly.

In the next chapter, we're going to deal with something just as real: Time Is a Thief— how delay, distraction, and "I'll get to it later" steal more vision than failure ever could, and how to bring urgency back without burning yourself—or your team—out.

GUARDING THE VISION: LEADERSHIP CHECKLIST

When I first stepped into a leadership role, I wished someone had handed me a tool for building alignment and driving execution. Over the years, I've refined the tools that made the biggest difference. Here's one you can use quarterly or biannually to keep your team focused and accountable.

Instructions

Review each item below. For each statement, check if you have addressed it in your leadership practice. Use the reflection prompts to guide your next steps.

Vision & Execution

- **Have I defined a clear, compelling vision for meaningful change in my organization?**
  Is my vision more than a slogan or a goal—does it inspire and guide real transformation?
- **Am I backing my vision with disciplined execution?**
  Are my actions, systems, and decisions aligned with the vision I communicate?

Communication & Alignment

- **Do I share my vision intentionally and strategically?**
  Have I started with self-reflection, tested with trusted advisors, and only then communicated broadly?

- **Am I modeling the change I want to see?**
  Are my behaviors consistent with the vision I've set?
- **Are my organization's systems and incentives aligned with our vision?**
  Do our structures support the vision, or is there a gap between what we say and what we do?

Testing & Evidence

- **Have I pressure-tested my vision before public rollout?**
  Did I use pilot projects and confidential feedback to strengthen ideas and anticipate challenges?
- **Am I communicating with evidence?**
  When I share the vision, do I show what's already started, what it's cost, and what's next?

Reflection & Adjustment

- **Do I regularly reflect on my approach to vision?**
  Am I protecting and building my vision, or just performing it for others?

Reflection Prompts

- What vision have I been talking about more than building?
- Where am I chasing the feeling of change instead of doing the work of change?
- Who are the two or three people I can trust to help pressure-test what I see?

- What's one vision I need to pull back from the public and quietly start constructing in private?

Use this checklist to guide your leadership journey. Revisit regularly to ensure your vision is protected, refined, and realized through disciplined action.

Chapter 5
Quiet Impact, Loud Legacy

In business, objectives don't move because people agree in meetings. They move because someone produces outcomes. You can have a clear strategy. You can have smart people. You can have the right slide deck. But at the end of the quarter, the only thing that really speaks is what got delivered—what improved, what got fixed, what got simplified, what shipped, what customers felt, what teams experienced. That's why the best leaders don't just talk about performance. They build a culture where results speak louder—consistently, quietly, and without needing a spotlight.

THE DIFFERENCE BETWEEN VISIBILITY AND VALUE

I didn't learn about true leadership from a manual or a seminar—I learned it from my Uncle Otoniel.

My uncle was the local radio guy. He came on every morning with the news. But he didn't treat that microphone like a stage. He treated it like a tool. If someone in the community needed a fridge, a bed, food—he would say it live on air. "Who can help?" Sometimes people stepped up. Sometimes nobody did. But the need still got met. Because if nobody moved, he moved. He'd locate the item. He'd deliver it himself. And if he had to, he'd buy it on credit—out of pocket—quietly. No announcement. No expectation of recognition. No "make sure you tell people it was me." While he was doing all of this, his own washer was held together with a rope. His own fridge barely worked. He didn't broadcast sacrifice. He didn't build his identity on being "the helper." He just did what needed to be done. That's leadership. The kind that holds weight and not just sounds good.

When he passed, the entire town of Coamo, Puerto Rico, didn't just show up; it paused. People filled the streets—not for a spectacle, but because their lives had quietly been changed. The funeral was so large it outgrew the chapel and spilled into the bus terminal. Schools closed. Shops locked their doors. One after another, people came to our family, sharing stories— not rehearsed, not exaggerated, just honest moments: groceries turning up when someone was desperate, a roof fixed after a storm, a child flown to receive surgery that changed everything. The most startling part? Most of us had no idea how much he'd done until he was gone.

That's when it hit me: legacy isn't something you announce. It's something revealed, often quietly, through the lives you touch. Uncle Otoniel never chased the spotlight—

he just showed up where it mattered. In today's work culture, we're quick to measure impact by who's loudest, who has the most updates, who's always in the room. And sure, communication and alignment are important. But alignment without action is just noise. My uncle's life exposes the hard truth organizations need to accept: visibility is not value. Value is measured by what truly gets better because you were there.

A NONPROFIT BUILT BEFORE CONVENIENCE EXISTED

In the early '90s—before the internet made everything easier—my uncle started an organization to help sick children get surgeries in the United States: Fundación Otoniel Olivieri. Here's the detail that matters: He didn't speak English. And it still didn't stop him. He found hospitals. He found pathways. He got on planes. Sometimes he brought a lawyer friend to translate. He figured it out as he went. That's "renewing your mind" in action: A renewed mind doesn't wait for perfect confidence. A renewed mind commits to the mission and builds competence along the way.

In business, people stall because they want certainty before action. But leadership often requires action before certainty—especially when the cost of waiting is too high.

HURRICANE SEASON EXPOSES LEADERSHIP

When the hurricane hit Puerto Rico, everything was chaos—power lines down, roofs torn apart, streets changed overnight. My uncle did what he always did: he organized. Contractors, roofers, and volunteers. He pulled people together and helped rebuild homes. He went where the need was greatest and started moving pieces into place. My Aunt, Lourdes, told me something that stayed with me: their own roof had a blue tarp for weeks. He kept saying, "We'll get to ours later. Others need help now." There's a leadership principle hiding in that sentence: A leader's priorities are revealed under pressure.

In organizations, you learn what leaders truly value when timelines tighten, customers complain, and tradeoffs become real. That's when values stop being words and start being choices.

After the storm, the streetlights eventually came back, but many homes were still without power. In the middle of that, there was a neighbor dealing with a medical condition that depended on electricity. No power meant real risk—immediate, not theoretical. My uncle had basic knowledge of how electricity worked, and in the urgency of the moment he tried to pull power from the pole to help that person. It was a tragic accident. He died attempting it.

I share that for one reason: not to dramatize it, but to clarify the kind of leader he was—someone who responded when the need was real. And it also reinforces a business truth leaders need to hear: a mission-driven heart is powerful, but sustainable impact requires systems, safeguards, and infrastructure so help doesn't depend on one person putting everything on their back. For business leaders, this means building processes and support structures that allow teams to respond to urgent needs without risking individual well-being or organizational stability.

THE MOMENT WE SAW THE "RECEIPTS"

At the funeral, the community's response was overwhelming. But then something else happened that exposed just how much my uncle had been carrying. His lawyer friend called the family and said Uncle Otoniel owed a large debt at the local appliance store. My aunt was confused. Their own appliances at home were barely hanging on. So why would he owe that much? And that's when we found out: Whenever he put a need on the radio and nobody responded, he would go buy the item himself— on a payment plan—and deliver it as if it was donated. No announcement.

That's when I understood a concept that every business leader should adopt: Receipts beat reports. Reports can be polished. To apply this in your organization, create rituals or review processes that focus on proof of delivery—actual outcomes, not just updates.

THE CORPORATE TRANSLATION: RESULTS SPEAK LOUDEST

Organizations love updates. Dashboards. Syncs. Status meetings. But here's the problem: it's possible to have a lot of communication and still have very little progress. A team can "talk about the objective" for months. But outcomes don't move from talk. They move from execution. This is why I call this chapter "Quiet Impact, Loud Legacy." Because the best leaders don't need to be the loudest voice in the room. They need to be the most consistent force behind outcomes.

Quiet impact looks like:

- a customer issue solved at the root (not patched)
- a process simplified so work becomes easier next month
- a new hire developed so performance compounds
- a problem removed so it doesn't return every week
- a decision made so teams don't stall in ambiguity
- a promise kept, even when it costs something

That is how credibility is built. That is how culture is shaped.

RENEWING YOUR MIND MEANS RENEWING YOUR SCOREBOARD

If you want a Factory Reset in your organization, you have to change what gets rewarded. Because what you reward, you reproduce. If you reward:

- visibility over delivery
- talk over proof
- busyness over outcomes
- heroics over systems

…you'll build a culture that looks active but doesn't move the needle.

If you reward:

- execution
- clarity
- problem-solving
- consistency
- measurable improvements

…you'll build a culture that compounds. My uncle didn't chase recognition. He chased impact. And the results spoke for him.

THE QUIET IMPACT LOOP

Here's the leadership pattern I took from his life and translated into business:

- See the need clearly (no denial, no minimizing)
- Own it (stop waiting for "someone")
- Deliver the solution (not discussion—action)
- Close the loop (confirm it truly helped)
- Build a system (so the solution becomes repeatable)

For leaders, that last step is key. The goal isn't to be the person who always fixes things. The goal is to build an environment where things get fixed faster and don't keep breaking the same way. To make this actionable, consider using a weekly checklist or template to track these steps for your team.

To embed this kind of lasting impact in your team—without turning your best people into the "go-to" fixers—consider implementing an Impact Ledger as your weekly scoreboard. This isn't about more meetings or extra paperwork; it's a simple, direct, and honest approach to shifting the team's focus from activity to actual improvement.

Here's how it works: each week, reflect on three straightforward questions as a group:

- Who did we help? (customer, teammate, partner)
- What did we fix? (root cause, recurring issue, bottleneck)

- What did we deliver? (measurable outcome, not just effort)

You'll be surprised how quickly this rhythm resets a team's culture, moving everyone from passive discussion to meaningful action.

To anchor this habit, try "Receipts Friday." For four weeks, close out every Friday by having each person share three crisp bullets:

- One delivered result—a tangible receipt of impact.
- One blocker removed—something that reduces friction for the future.
- One decision needed—to keep momentum protected and priorities clear.

No essays. No fluff. Just proof. This practice turns execution into a weekly rhythm and makes outcomes the shared language of your team.

My uncle's legacy wasn't built on what he talked about—it was built on what he quietly and consistently did, often at real personal cost. After he passed, the community didn't remember him for his words; they remembered him because their lives were tangibly better for having known him. That's the quiet impact loop in action. Adopt these habits, and you'll see the same kind of legacy start to take root—not in what you say, but in what truly improves because of you.

That's the reset. If you want to renew your mind as a leader, here's the standard: Stop measuring yourself by how visible you are. Start measuring yourself by what improves because of you. Quiet impact creates loud legacy—every time. Let your results speak louder than any words you can speak.

KEY TAKEAWAYS

- Results Speak Louder Than Words: True leadership is measured by outcomes, not by visibility or talk.
- Legacy Is Revealed, Not Announced: The most impactful leaders often work behind the scenes, letting their results build their reputation.
- Visibility ≠ Value: Don't confuse activity or presence with genuine progress. Value is what improves because you were there.
- Systems Over Heroics: Sustainable impact requires building systems and safeguards, not relying on individual heroics.
- Receipts Beat Reports: Proof of delivery (receipts) is more powerful than polished updates (reports).
- Weekly Scoreboard: Track who you helped, what you fixed, and what you delivered each week to reinforce a culture of execution.
- Renew Your Scoreboard: Reward execution, clarity, problem-solving, and consistency to build a culture that compounds.
- Reflect Regularly: Ask yourself and your team, "What improved because of us? To keep the focus on impact.

Chapter 6
Execution Has a Beat

Before I ever led a sales team—before the conference rooms, dashboards, and "alignment" calls—I learned leadership in a place where guessing wasn't an option. My first lessons came as a bouncer, standing near the stage at live salsa shows. The energy was real, and the problems showed up fast. In that environment, leadership wasn't about talking—it was about reading the room, feeling the temperature, and acting early so issues never became a scene.

That's leadership: not loud, not dramatic, but aware, steady, and on time. The best execution I've seen in business feels exactly like the best live band I've ever stood next to.

NOISE VS. MUSIC: THE FOUNDATION OF EXECUTION

If you've ever been close to a live salsa band, you know the difference between noise and music. When the rhythm section is locked in, the whole room locks in. The horns shine, the singer works the crowd, and the dancers move effortlessly. But if the beat is off—even for a moment—the best bands don't freeze.

They listen, adjust, and improvise. The conga player might throw in a fill, the singer might riff, and suddenly, the groove returns. That's recovery: quick, quiet, and essential.

Business works the same way. You can have smart people, strong strategy, and big objectives, but if the cadence is chaotic—priorities shifting, decisions vague, meetings multiplying—your team starts operating like a band with no steady rhythm. Effort alone isn't enough. Execution has a beat, and when it slips, leaders must help the team find it again.

THE HIDDEN COSTS OF SILOS: NOISY BANDS

Most corporations get jammed up when every division becomes its own band. Sales, Marketing, Ops, Product, Legal, Finance, Support—each has its rhythm. Excellence in isolation can still produce a mess. That's the sound of silos: lots of activity, meetings, and stress, but not enough clean outcomes. It's usually a rhythm problem, not a talent problem.

Leaders often underestimate silos. They don't just slow work—they change behavior. Silos create distance, and once there's distance, people start protecting themselves. The goal shifts from "make the outcome win" to "make my part look good." Blame management replaces results management. Hand-offs become hot potatoes, information gets hoarded, and meetings become protection rather than progress. The worst version? The customer becomes the messenger between departments. When silos change behavior, even talented people look average because their energy is spent clarifying confusion, defending boundaries, and avoiding blame instead of building outcomes. Silo problems feel like culture because they are.

But when an organization locks in, it's something to watch. Divisions stop playing solo and start moving together. Work stacks clean, decisions speed up, duplication disappears, and the customer experience gets smoother. Stress drops, and it feels like one band. You stop hearing, "Who owns this?" or "Are we aligned?" When the beat is right, people know what matters and what time it is—no daily speeches required.

LEADERSHIP: THE CONDUCTOR'S ROLE

Leadership isn't about being the loudest in the room. It's about keeping the rhythm steady. A conductor doesn't tell the orchestra to play louder; a conductor knows the sound, what needs to stay steady, what needs to come forward, what needs space, and what needs to hit on time. Great leaders do the same with teams: knowing who needs pressure, who needs confidence, who needs recognition, who needs quiet respect, who needs structure, and who needs room. One leadership style won't move everybody.

Leading sales teams taught me that motivation isn't one message. Some reps respond to commission, some to recognition, some to family. Same quota, same product, same floor—different reasons, different rhythm. So, I coached differently, not to be inspirational, but to get the best out of the people I had. When you do that, people bring their real strength to the table instead of protecting themselves.

THE REAL EXECUTION KILLER: UNSTABLE TEMPO

Many leaders spend most of their time fixing weaknesses. There's a place for that, but you win faster by positioning people in their strengths and putting guardrails around what can trip them up. In music, you don't force the conga player to be a trumpet player. You let them control rhythm and build around it. Same in business: some people are closers, some builders, planners, stabilizers, relationship engines, detail assassins. If you don't know what instrument you're holding, you can't make great music.

Even with great people, execution breaks when the tempo keeps changing. Teams can handle hard work, but constant rhythm changes—shifting priorities, unclear ownership, urgent requests, delayed decisions, reopened work—drain them. It's like trying to dance salsa while the DJ keeps switching the song every 30 seconds. People lose trust, not because leadership is evil, but because the rhythm is unreliable. Once trust drops, execution gets expensive.

IMPROVISATION: THE ART OF GETTING BACK ON BEAT

In music, mistakes happen. The best bands don't dwell—they recover. Someone steps up, fills the gap, and the song keeps moving. In business, recovery is just as critical. When priorities shift or a project stumbles, great teams don't point fingers—they improvise, adapt, and get back in sync.

Leaders set the tone for recovery. If you panic, the team panics. If you adjust calmly, the team finds its rhythm. The goal isn't perfection—it's resilience. The ability to improvise, recover, and keep the beat steady is what separates good teams from great ones.

THE BEAT THAT MAKES EXECUTION INEVITABLE

I learned on those club stages that the room changes when the rhythm is right. In corporate leadership, the same is true. The best teams don't win because they talk more. They win because they lock in. They share a beat, leverage strengths, keep the tempo steady, and execute like one band.

Execution needs a repeatable cadence that answers five questions every week:

1. What matters most right now?
2. Who owns it?
3. What does "done" mean—exactly?
4. What are we not doing this week so we can do this well?
5. How are we proving progress without drowning in meetings?

When those answers are clear, the band locks in. When they're fuzzy, it turns into noise.

If you want better execution, don't start with more pressure. Start with better rhythm. When execution has a beat, you don't have to sell people on progress—the results speak for themselves.

KEY TAKEAWAYS

- Execution thrives on rhythm, not just effort.
- Silos create noise and change behavior; alignment creates music and results.
- Leadership is about keeping the beat steady, not being the loudest.
- Leverage individual strengths and motivations—don't flatten people.
- A repeatable cadence and clear answers drive inevitable execution.
- Lead like a conductor: balance, timing, and awareness unlock team performance.

A PRACTICAL TOOL: THE INSTRUMENT MAP

Here's a simple tool to bring rhythm to your team:

- Write down each key person and answer:

  - What are they naturally strong at?

  - What motivates them most—money, mastery, recognition, mission, stability, growth?

  - What rhythm do they need—structure, autonomy, competition, coaching, quiet focus?

Then lead like a conductor: don't overplay the horns, don't mute the rhythm section, don't rush the tempo, and don't leave your best instrument sitting silent.

INSTRUMENT MAP TEMPLATE

Purpose: Capture each team member's strengths, motivations, and rhythm needs, so you can lead like a conductor and build a team that "locks in" together.

HOW TO USE

1. List each key person on your team.
2. Fill in their strengths, motivators, and rhythm needs.
3. Add notes for yourself as the leader—how to bring out their best.
4. Review the map regularly and adjust as people grow or roles change.

Team Member	Natural Strengths	Motivators	Rhythm Needs	Notes for the Conductor
Name	*What do they do best? (e.g., closer, planner, relationship builder, detail assassin)*	*What drives them? (e.g., money, mastery, recognition, mission, stability, growth)*	*What environment helps them thrive? (e.g., structure, autonomy, competition, coaching, quiet focus)*	*How should you lead them? (e.g., give space, apply pressure, offer recognition, provide structure)*

Example Entry

Team Member	Natural Strengths	Motivators	Rhythm Needs	Notes for the Conductor
Alex	*Relationship engine, builder*	*Recognition, growth*	*Coaching, autonomy*	*Celebrate wins publicly, check in regularly, let them run with new ideas*

Chapter 7
No More Hero Mode

In school, many of us mastered a habit that's hard to shake: wait until the last minute, cram, pass the test, move on. You pull an all-nighter, fuel up on caffeine, and somehow—by sheer adrenaline—you survive. Sometimes you even feel proud: "Look at me, I pulled it off."

But business isn't graded on effort. It's graded on results—and not just any results, but *quality*. Your "test" isn't a multiple-choice exam. It's a customer. A contract. An implementation. A launch. A reputation. And you can't cram quality. You can cram information, slides, activity. But you can't cram trust.

This chapter is about why last-minute heroics are a broken system—and how leaders can reset their organizations for lasting success.

THE CORPORATE VERSION OF CRAMMING

Let's name what "cramming" looks like in business—especially in technology:

- A deal closes… and implementation finds out late.

- Onboarding starts… but nobody documented what was promised.
- The customer goes live… but training is rushed.
- A big launch happens… but support wasn't prepared.
- An escalation hits… and now everybody's scrambling.
- Leadership asks for answers… and everyone starts collecting screenshots.
- The team is "busy" all week but finishes everything Friday at 6:45 PM.

That's cramming. It's just wearing a badge that says, "high performer." The worst part? It becomes cultural. People start accepting chaos as normal: "This is just how we operate." "We move fast." "We're lean." "We're in growth mode."

But that's not speed. That's a system that doesn't protect quality. Speed is clean. Chaos is loud.

WHY HERO MODE FEELS GOOD… UNTIL IT DOESN'T

Hero mode is addictive because it delivers quick emotional pay-offs. When someone saves the day at the last minute, they get praised, get attention, feel needed, feel important, and feel like the glue holding it all together. Leaders—often unconsciously—reward this behavior. They celebrate the firefighter, not the fire prevention.

So, the team learns: don't fix the system—be the hero.

But here's the bill that always comes due: Hero mode makes the company fragile. If one person is "the closer," "the fixer," "the one who knows everything," then the business is operating on one knee. It's only a matter of time before the hero gets sick, goes on vacation, quits, or burns out. Then everybody panics and realizes the truth: You didn't have a process. You had a person. That's not a strategy. That's a gamble.

THE QUIET COST NOBODY TALKS ABOUT

Last-minute culture quietly undermines your organization:

- **It punishes planners.** People who try to plan ahead get ignored until the problem is urgent. Then they get blamed: "Why didn't we see this coming?"—when they did.
- **It rewards loudness.** Whoever yells first gets resources, not who has the clearest case or biggest impact.
- **It makes people hide problems.** Raising issues early feels risky, so people stay quiet until the issue is unavoidable.
- **It trains teams to accept sloppy handoffs.** "We'll figure it out" becomes the operating principle, sinking more implementations than any competitor ever did.

Want to know if your culture is in hero mode? Listen for: "It is what it is," "We'll make it work," "Just get it done," or "We'll clean it up later." Later rarely comes.

SILOS MAKE CRAMMING WORSE

Silos don't just slow work—they change behavior, especially under pressure. Silos create distance. Once there's distance, people stop moving like one team and start moving like separate survival units.

Here's how it shows up:

- People own their piece, not the whole. The goal becomes "make my part look good," not "make the outcome win."

- Blame management replaces results management. "We sent it to them." "We're waiting on approval." "That's not in our scope." "We followed process." All true, but execution is breaking down.

- Handoffs become hot potatoes. Work gets thrown over the wall. The next team catches it late, confused, and frustrated. Then they do the same to the next team.

- Information becomes currency. In healthy environments, information moves fast. In siloed environments, it gets

hoarded. Teams hold back details, leading to late surprises—
and surprises are expensive.

- Meetings become protection, not progress. Meetings are
  scheduled to create a paper trail, not to solve problems. Calendars fill up, outcomes slow down.

- Customers become messengers. When a customer has to
  carry the story from Sales to Support to Ops to Billing, your
  company is telling them, "We don't have one beat."

Silo problems aren't just workflow—they're culture.

THE BIG RESET: STOP TRYING TO PASS AND START DELIVERING

This is the mindset shift. In school, you can pass a test and forget the material next week. In business, you can't "pass" and
forget the damage.

If the customer has to call you three times after go-live,
you didn't pass. If your implementation creates ten new support tickets, you didn't pass. If your sales team is selling dreams
your delivery team can't fulfill, you didn't pass. If your support
team is constantly apologizing, you didn't pass. If renewals are
dropping because onboarding was sloppy, you didn't pass.

In business, passing isn't the goal. Delivering is the goal.

Delivering means:

- Clean handoffs
- Clear expectations
- Documented commitments
- Real adoption
- Stable outcomes
- Fewer surprises

A customer who says, "That was smooth." What does a reset look like? It's moving from "Who can save this?" to "How do we prevent this?" It's moving from personality-based execution to system-based execution.

You don't build a strong operation by hoping people will "figure it out." You build a strong operation by making the path clear enough that people can execute it consistently. That's not bureaucracy; it's effective leadership. To fix the silo mentality and provide clarity to your team, there are four steps you can take to move toward clear expectations.

FOUR MOVES THAT FIX SILO MENTALITY

Here's a framework to help you move from silos to proactive operational thinking. No fancy words. Just the real work:

1) Simplify

Cut the noise. If you have five approval steps and three add no value, cut them. If every deal is custom, tighten packaging. If you're tracking ten KPIs but only two drive outcomes, focus. Complexity doesn't make you sophisticated. Complexity makes you slow and fragile.

CASE STUDY: SIMPLIFYING FOR SPEED AND IMPACT

Background:

A mid-sized SaaS company was struggling with slow project delivery. Every new customer implementation required five separate approval steps—legal, finance, product, operations, and executive sign-off. Each step added delays, confusion, and frustration. Teams spent more time chasing signatures than serving customers.

The Move:

Leadership decided to audit the approval process. They discovered that three of the five steps added little value and were mostly legacy requirements. By eliminating redundant approvals and empowering project managers to make decisions within clear guardrails, they cut the process down to two essential steps.

The Result:

- Project delivery times dropped by 30%.
- Customer onboarding became smoother and faster.
- Teams spent less time in "waiting mode" and more time focused on outcomes.
- Employee satisfaction improved—people felt trusted to execute.

Key Insight:

Simplifying wasn't about cutting corners. It was about removing noise so teams could deliver quality work, faster. Complexity didn't make the company sophisticated—it made it slow and fragile.

2) Standardize

Write it down. Not a 40-page manual nobody reads—a simple playbook. A playbook answers: what do we do first, what comes next, who owns what, what "good" looks like, what to do when things go wrong. Standardizing stops you from re-learning the same lesson every week.

CASE STUDY: MID-SIZE SAAS COMPANY STANDARDIZES ONBOARDING

Background:

A mid-sized SaaS company was experiencing slow onboarding for new customer success managers. Each department had its own onboarding checklist, leading to confusion, missed steps, and inconsistent training. New hires often felt lost, and managers spent excessive time clarifying procedures and correcting errors.

The Move:

The People Operations and Customer Success teams collaborated to create a single, one-page onboarding playbook. This document outlined the essential steps for a new manager's first week: system access, product training, customer engagement protocols, and escalation procedures. The playbook was visually simple, easy to reference, and included clear ownership for each step.

The Result:

- Onboarding time for new customer success managers dropped by 35%.
- Training errors and missed steps decreased significantly.
- New hires reported feeling more confident and supported.

- Managers spent less time troubleshooting and more time coaching and developing talent.

Key Insight:

A concise, standardized playbook replaced confusion with clarity. By focusing on what mattered most, the team ensured every new hire started strong, and the onboarding experience became consistent and scalable across the SaaS organization.

3) Support

Give people the tools and enablement to execute. Standardizing without support is just rules people ignore. Support looks like: training that matches real scenarios, templates that make good work easier, checklists that protect quality under pressure, dashboards that show what's stuck early, a clear escalation path that doesn't turn into drama. Support makes the standard livable.

CASE STUDY: CREATE TOOLS TO REDUCE IMPLEMENTATION ERRORS

Background:

A fast-growing SaaS provider specializing in workflow automation noticed a surge in implementation errors during periods of rapid client onboarding. Project teams were juggling multiple deployments, and under pressure, critical configuration steps were often missed. This led to delayed launches, increased support tickets, and frustrated customers.

The Move:

The company's operations and product teams collaborated to develop digital checklists for every major implementation phase—requirements gathering, system setup, data migration, and client training. These checklists were integrated into the project management platform, making them accessible and mandatory for each deployment. Training sessions were updated to include real-world troubleshooting scenarios, and a dedicated support channel was launched for instant help during go-live events.

The Result:

- Implementation errors dropped by 50%.
- Project managers and engineers reported greater confidence and less stress.
- Customer satisfaction scores improved, with fewer complaints about onboarding.
- Teams handled higher volumes without sacrificing quality or morale.

Key Insight:

Support wasn't just about adding resources—it was about making it easy for teams to deliver excellence, even under pressure. Digital checklists and real-time support transformed best practices into daily habits, driving consistent results and happier customers.

4) Scale

Make the operation transferable. If you can't onboard a new person without months of shadowing, you don't have a system—you have tribal knowledge. Scaling means: new hires ramp faster, quality stays consistent, customers get the same experience regardless of who's assigned, the company doesn't fall apart when one person leaves. That's real growth.

CASE STUDY: SCALING ONBOARDING WITH DIGITAL CHECKLISTS IN SAAS

Background:

A rapidly expanding SaaS company specializing in cloud-based analytics was struggling to onboard new implementation specialists efficiently. As the company grew, knowledge was siloed among veteran staff, and new hires took months to reach full productivity. This bottleneck slowed customer deployments and limited the company's ability to scale.

The Move:

Leadership built on the success of digital checklists used in implementation by creating a comprehensive onboarding portal. This portal included step-by-step digital checklists for every onboarding phase—company orientation, product deep-dives, customer workflow simulations, and troubleshooting labs. Each checklist was interactive, tracked progress, and linked to real-time support channels. The onboarding process was standardized and regularly updated based on feedback from new hires and team leads.

The Result:

- New implementation specialists reached full productivity 40% faster.
- Customer deployments accelerated, supporting the company's growth targets.
- Quality and consistency improved across teams and regions.
- Managers spent less time on repetitive training and more time developing advanced skills.
- The company scaled rapidly without sacrificing standards or customer satisfaction.

Key Insight:

Scaling wasn't just about hiring more people—it was about making expertise accessible and processes repeatable. Digital checklists and a standardized onboarding system turned rapid growth from a challenge into a competitive advantage.

THE TECH-SALES HANDOFF: WHERE IT BREAKS THE MOST

If you sell tech, you already know where the pain lives: The handoff. Sales closes the deal. Implementation inherits the promise. Support inherits the outcome. Do those teams move like one band—or like three separate bands who barely talk?

A clean organization has a handoff that's tight:

- What was sold is documented in plain language
- Customer expectations are clear
- The timeline is realistic
- Risks are flagged early
- Success metrics are defined up front
- The customer's responsibilities are stated clearly
- Implementation knows what they're walking into

A messy organization has a handoff that vibes:

- "I think they wanted this feature."
- "We'll figure it out as we go."
- "The customer is a little confused, but we'll handle it."
- "We promised it, so we gotta make it work."

That's hero mode.

A TOOL YOU CAN USE: THE NO-CRAMMING CHECKLIST

School taught a lot of us how to cram. But business will humble you if you try to run operations like a last-minute test. Customers don't grade you on effort. They grade you on outcomes—and how smooth it felt to get there. Before implementation starts, confirm:

- What exactly was sold (in plain language)
- What timeline was promised
- What success looks like (measurable outcomes)
- Who owns the customer relationship now
- What risks exist (data, integrations, approvals, training)
- What the customer must do on their side
- What the first milestone is, with a real date
- What the "go-live" definition is (no moving goalposts)
- What support needs to know before launch

This checklist doesn't slow you down. It speeds you up—because it prevents the Friday-night scramble.

Now imagine an organization where every team moves in sync, where handoffs are seamless, and where customers rave about their experience—not because someone pulled off a last-minute miracle, but because excellence is built into the system from day one. Picture a workplace where leaders empower their teams to prevent fires instead of celebrating the firefighter, where growth is sustainable, and where people thrive without burning out.

This is not just operational discipline—it's a culture shift. When you move beyond hero mode and invest in resilient systems, you unlock the true potential of your business. You create an environment where results are consistent, surprises are rare, and every Friday feels like a win—not a rescue mission.

The future belongs to organizations that deliver, not just survive. Build your company to scale, to adapt, and to win— week after week, year after year. That's the reset. That's leadership. And that's how you grow without needing miracles.

KEY TAKEAWAYS

- Hero mode is unsustainable; systems and processes drive lasting success.
- Silos and last-minute culture undermine quality and trust.
- Leaders must champion simplification, standardization, support, and scalability.
- Clean handoffs and clear documentation prevent chaos and protect outcomes.
- The No-Cramming Checklist is a practical tool for operational excellence.

Chapter 8
The Reset Code

Let's land this plane the right way—not with a mic-drop, not with hype that fades by Tuesday morning. You know that energy: everyone clapping, fired up… then the calendar flips and it's back to old habits.

We're closing with something stronger than motivation: a standard. Inspiration is a spark. A standard is a system. And systems don't care if you woke up tired, stressed, or juggling ten things at once. Systems run regardless.

This book is about *Factory Reset*—renewing your mind and your leadership. In business, that means you stop running on default settings: reactive, busy, always catching up, always "we'll get to it." You start operating with intention. You lead with clarity. You execute with rhythm. You let your results speak.

Here's the final truth: If your reset isn't repeatable, it isn't real. This chapter is your code—the operating system you can bring into Monday morning and actually use.

FIVE RULES TO THE RESET CODE

A reset isn't a speech you give your team. It's how you run your week when nobody's watching. It starts with five rules. Simple. Not easy—but simple.

Rule 1: One Objective

Most teams don't lose because they don't work hard. They lose because they try to win ten games at once. The fastest way to kill execution is to call everything a priority. When everything matters, nothing moves.

Standard:

Pick one objective that matters most right now. Not one per department—one for the team. This doesn't mean the rest of the business disappears. It means the team knows what gets protected when pressure hits and people start pulling you in every direction. One objective is focus. Focus is speed.

Leadership Tip: Tie your objective to a measurable business outcome—revenue, customer satisfaction, or operational efficiency. Share a real example: "During our product launch, our single objective was customer adoption. Every decision supported that."

Rule 2: Clear Owners

Want to expose a weak operation fast? Listen for this sentence: "Someone should…" That's a reset opportunity. "Someone" is how good ideas die.

Clear ownership turns plans into outcomes. Not committees. Not long email chains. Not "we all agree." Every priority needs a name next to it—not a team name, a person. Owners aren't the person who does all the work; they're accountable for the outcome—driving clarity, removing blockers, and making sure things finish clean. No owners? Be honest: it's not happening.

Leadership Tip: Empower owners to make decisions and learn from outcomes. Accountability drives growth at every level.

Rule 3: Protected Build Time

If your calendar is all meetings, your results will be all talk. Teams don't need more syncs. They need more time to build, solve, deliver, and finish. In tech, you can't "meeting" your way into outcomes.

Standard:

Protect build time like it's revenue—because it is. Meetings aren't evil, but they're expensive. If you're meeting all week, you're spending your execution budget on conversation and calling it progress. Good leaders don't just schedule meetings. They schedule momentum.

Leadership Tip: Show how protected build time led to faster delivery or higher quality in your organization.

Rule 4: Weekly Receipts

This is where you separate activity from progress. A lot of teams run hard and still can't point to what moved forward. Everything sounds like: "We're working on it." "We had a good meeting." "We're close." Okay… but what changed?

Every week needs receipts. Not a report. Not a deck. Receipts. Did the contract get signed? Did procurement clear it? Did the decision maker say yes—with a real date, not vibes? Did we move the deal forward in a way that's irreversible? Did we deliver the implementation—or are we still "in progress"? Did the tech go live, or is it sitting in staging? Did the customer adopt it, or are they stuck and quiet? Did we hit the milestone, or did we just talk about the milestone? Did the customer get value fast, or did we hand them a login and pray?

That's tech execution. Progress isn't "we met." Progress is: the customer committed, the solution launched, and the outcome improved. Weekly receipts keep the organization honest.

They keep leaders honest too—because you can't hide behind motion when receipts are the standard.

DEFINING PROGRESS THROUGH WEEKLY RECEIPTS

True execution in technology isn't measured by the number of meetings held or conversations had; it's reflected in tangible outcomes. Progress means the customer has made a commitment, the solution has been launched, and there has been noticeable improvement in results.

Implementing weekly receipts is essential for maintaining transparency and accountability within the organization. These receipts act as proof of progress and ensure that both the team and its leaders remain honest about what has truly moved forward. By making receipts the standard, it eliminates the possibility of hiding behind busyness or mere activity, and instead demands real evidence of advancement.

Leadership Tip: Use a simple checklist or dashboard to track weekly receipts. Make it visible to the team.

Rule 5: Systems Over Heroics

This is the final upgrade—the grown-leader move. A lot of companies survive on heroics: one person always saving the day, staying late, cleaning up the mess, pushing the boulder uphill. It looks impressive... until it breaks the person and exposes the operation.

Standard:

Don't celebrate heroics. Replace the need for heroics. If something keeps happening, it's not a surprise anymore—it's a system problem. System problems need system solutions: better handoffs, clearer decision rights, fewer approvals, stronger checklists, cleaner workflows. Impact that depends on one person is fragile. Impact built into a system is scalable.

Leadership Tip: Share how a system changes reduced burnout and improved team resilience.

THE 90-DAY RESET PLAN

Standards are great, but you might be thinking: "Alright Manny... where do I start?" Here's the simplest 90-day plan I know—built for real life, not perfect conditions.

Days 1–30: Reset Clarity

- Pick the one objective you're driving.
- Identify the top three priorities that move it.
- Assign clear owners.
- Define what "done" means.

- Cut the noise: pause anything that doesn't support the objective.

Clarity forces tradeoffs, but it brings peace back to teams.

Days 31–60: Reset Cadence

- Run a weekly operating cadence: decide, build, prove.
- Protect build time.
- Shrink meetings that don't produce decisions or receipts.
- Remove blockers fast—don't let them sit there like a brick wall.

Execution stops being emotional and starts being predictable.

Days 61–90: Reset Culture

- Weekly receipts become normal.
- Ownership becomes non-negotiable.
- Silos lose power because outcomes matter more than territory.
- Systems replace heroics.

By the end of 90 days, the goal isn't perfection. The goal is a team that feels different: clearer, steadier, faster, more confident, less chaotic. (See the "90-Day Reset Plan Template" at the end of this chapter.)

THE LEADERSHIP MIRROR

Now let's talk to the leader reading this—because this is where the reset gets personal. If you're serious about renewing your mind, you can't just reset the team. You have to reset yourself.

Here's the mirror. Ask yourself these questions straight:

- Am I creating clarity—or confusion with constant changes?
- Do I make decisions—or delay them and call it "alignment"?
- Do I protect build time—or fill calendars to feel in control?
- Do I reward receipts—or reward visibility?
- Do I build systems—or secretly enjoy being the one everybody needs?

Sometimes people don't fix the system because being needed feels good. But being needed isn't the goal. Being effective is.

Leadership Tip: Share your reflections with a trusted peer or coach. Transparency drives growth.

THE FINAL RESET

A Factory Reset is not a moment. It's a commitment to operate at a higher standard—especially when it's inconvenient. It's choosing outcomes over noise, rhythm over chaos, systems over ego, receipts over talk. If you do that consistently, you won't need to explain who you are as a leader. Your results will do it for you.

Don't tell people what you're going to do. Don't sell the dream and disappear. Build it. Close it. Implement it. Make it real. Repeat it. Because in the end—your results are your receipt. Make them loud.

KEY TAKEAWAYS

- **Set One Objective:** Focus your team on a single, high-impact goal to drive clarity and speed.
- **Assign Clear Ownership:** Ensure every priority has a named owner accountable for outcomes, not just tasks.
- **Protect Build Time:** Guard time for deep work and execution; minimize meetings that don't produce decisions or results.
- **Demand Weekly Receipts:** Track real progress with tangible outcomes, not just activity or discussion.
- **Build Systems, Not Heroics:** Design processes that scale and sustain results, reducing reliance on individual effort.
- **Follow the 90-Day Reset Plan:** Move through clarity, cadence, and culture to embed new standards and rhythms.
- **Reflect and Lead by Example:** Use the Leadership Mirror to assess your own habits and model the standards you expect.
- **Let Results Speak:** Consistent execution and outcomes will define your leadership more than words or promises.

90-DAY RESET PLAN TEMPLATE

The "90-Day Reset Plan" is a practical framework designed to help leaders and teams renew their focus, improve execution, and embed lasting cultural change. Instead of relying on motivation or temporary fixes, this plan emphasizes clear objectives, ownership, disciplined routines, and systems that drive consistent results.

The template breaks the reset process into three actionable phases—*Clarity, Cadence*, and *Culture*—making it easy to track progress and ensure that new standards become part of everyday operations. Share your reflections with a peer for accountability, and use the notes section to capture insights and lessons learned along the way.

Phase 1: Days 1–30 — Reset Clarity

Objective: Establish clear focus and ownership.

Action Step	Owner	Due Date	Status	Notes
Define the single, top-priority objective				
Identify top 3 priorities to drive objective				
Assign clear owners for each priority				
Define what "done" means for each priority				
Pause or defer non-essential activities				

Phase 2: Days 31–60 — Reset Cadence

Objective: Build operating rhythm and momentum.

Action Step	Owner	Due Date	Status	Notes
Establish weekly operating cadence (decide, build, prove)				
Schedule and protect build time				
Reduce meetings that don't produce decisions or receipts				
Remove blockers quickly				

Phase 3: Days 61–90 — Reset Culture

Objective: Embed standards and systems into team culture.

Action Step	Owner	Due Date	Status	Notes
Make weekly receipts a team norm				
Reinforce ownership as non-negotiable				
Break down silos—focus on outcomes				
Replace heroics with scalable systems				

Leadership Mirror (Self-Reflection)

- Am I creating clarity or confusion?
- Do I make timely decisions?
- Do I protect build time?
- Do I reward outcomes or visibility?

- Do I build systems or rely on heroics?

Tip: Review and discuss your reflections with a peer or coach for accountability.

Progress Tracking

- Review this template weekly.
- Update status and notes for each action step.
- Celebrate completed milestones and receipts.
- Adjust priorities as needed based on team feedback and results.

www.ingramcontent.com/pod-product-compliance
Lightning Source LLC
Chambersburg PA
CBHW031905200326
41597CB00012B/536